# EBELSKIVERS

recipes  **Kevin Crafts**

photographs  **Erin Kunkel**

weldon**owen**

# contents

# all about ebelskivers

Ebelskivers—light, puffy, sphere-shaped pancakes—are served with flavorful toppings and fillings. Incredibly versatile, they can be varied in countless delicious ways.

Ebelskivers (pronounced "able-skeevers") are originally from Denmark, served there as a traditional snack or dessert. Although the word "ebelskiver" (also spelled *aebleskiver*) literally translates to "sliced apples," these light, airy treats are more often found today simply dusted with confectioners' sugar and accompanied by fruit jam, such as raspberry or strawberry, or fruit curd.

Ebelskivers require little more than ingredients you probably already have on hand in your kitchen—milk, eggs, flour—and a special seven-welled pan that forms the pancakes' unique shape. The batter is a breeze to make, and the cooking method is so simple to master that it is easy to be creative when making ebelskivers. Modern versions can be sweet or savory, filled or unfilled, and feature fresh fruit or vegetables, preserves, caramel, chocolate, cheese, meat, and even seafood.

This book offers more than forty recipes for these tiny treats, perfect for a kid-friendly breakfast, an innovative snack, a conversation-sparking hors d'oeuvre, a light supper accompanied by a green salad, or an over-the-top dessert. The possibilities are endless!

# ebelskivers past & present

**THE LEGEND OF EBELSKIVERS**

The invention of ebelskivers is much debated, but one story tells of the Vikings returning very hungry from a fierce battle. With no frying pans on which to cook, they placed their damaged shields over a hot fire and cooked pancakes in the indentations.

Denmark's rich farmland is well suited to producing the grain and dairy products that form the basis of the ebelskiver batter. The country is also famous for its apples *(ebler)* that are the root of the word "ebelskiver."

Tracing their origin back for hundreds of years, ebelskivers are traditional fare at Danish holiday gatherings—especially Christmas—and at other family and community events. The distinctive pans for cooking the pancakes are family heirlooms, passed down from generation to generation (for more on ebelskiver pans, turn to page 11).

## dozens of varieties

While the literal translation of ebelskiver, "sliced apples," evokes an apple-filled pancake, every Danish household has its own unique recipe, and it may not include apples at all. Some use regular milk in the batter, while others favor buttermilk. Some families use baking powder for leavening, while others feel yeast produces a better flavor. One cook might scent the batter with cardamom, another with nutmeg. One grandmother might serve her treasured recipe with applesauce, while her daughter might offer raspberry jam to her guests.

For today's cooks, this spirit of customizing the ebelskiver according to one's own taste is appealing, thanks to the ease of making and cooking the pancakes. The following pages offer a variety of inspiration—from the traditional to the fanciful—to spark your imagination.

# equipment

Aside from the traditional pan, making ebelskivers does not require special equipment. Measuring tools, a whisk, and silicone spatula are the minimum tools needed to make the batter, but an electric mixer will make quick work of beating the egg whites, which are responsible for the light and airy texture of the pancakes. A couple of wooden skewers or thin icing spatulas—even knitting needles—help flip the pancakes efficiently and easily (see page 14 for detailed instructions).

## the ebelskiver pan

Most of the ebelskiver pans available today are 9 to 10 inches in diameter and feature the traditional round shape with seven deep, hemispherical wells for the batter and a long handle. You can also find rectangular pans with nine wells. Traditional pans are made from cast iron and require seasoning in order to obtain a stick-resistant finish over time. Some heirloom pans are made from copper, but they are troublesome to cook with. You can find these traditional pans in flea markets and antique stores, reflecting the historical significance of ebelskivers in Danish households.

Modern-style ebelskiver pans are made from cast aluminum, which heats quickly and evenly. Many also offer a nonstick coating on the pan surface to assure clean release of the pancakes, especially if the filling spills onto the pan. Modern ebelskiver pans are widely available in kitchenware stores or through Internet and mail-order sources.

**PAN TYPES**

If you are purchasing a traditional-style ebelskiver pan, be sure to buy the type that is best suited to your kitchen stove, as the pans are constructed a bit differently for gas stoves and electric models. Modern-style pans work on both types of appliances.

# making the batter

Ebelskivers are easy to make, requiring few ingredients and simple techniques. If working with egg whites seems daunting at first, don't worry: the batter is very forgiving.

1 **Mix the dry ingredients**  In a large bowl, whisk together the flour, sugar, baking powder, and salt. The recipe may also call for ground nuts, cornmeal, poppy seeds, or a dry flavoring in this step.

2 **Mix the wet ingredients**  In a small bowl, lightly whisk the egg yolks, then whisk in the milk, melted butter, and liquid flavorings, such as vanilla extract, peanut butter, or another flavoring called for in the recipe.

3 **Combine the dry and wet ingredients**  Add the yolk mixture to the bowl with the flour mixture. Switch to a wooden spoon and stir until the ingredients are well blended. The batter will appear slightly lumpy.

4 **Beat the egg whites**  In a clean bowl, using an electric mixer set on high speed, beat the egg whites until stiff, but not dry, peaks form. When the beaters are lifted, the egg whites should hold a firm peak that droops slightly at the top.

5 **Lighten the batter**  Pile about a third of the beaten egg whites on top of the batter. Using a rubber spatula, slice down through the center of the mixtures, then pull the spatula up along the side of the bowl and over the top, gently incorporating the two mixtures. Rotate the bowl a quarter turn and repeat until the egg whites have been incorporated.

6 **Finish the batter**  Repeat this folding action with the remaining beaten egg whites until no white streaks remain, taking care not to deflate the batter too much. Fold in any other ingredients called for in the recipe. Use the batter right away.

# filling & cooking ebelskivers

Creating luscious filled pancakes is easier than it looks. You'll want to work quickly to ensure the pancakes cook evenly, but the filling, cooking, and flipping are a breeze.

1 Butter the pan  Using a pastry brush, coat the wells of the ebelskiver pan evenly with melted butter and place over medium or medium-low heat, depending on the recipe. Let the butter heat for a few moments.

2 Add the batter  When the butter begins to bubble in the pan, use a 1-ounce ice cream scoop or two soupspoons (one spoon to scoop and one spoon to scrape) to add 1 to 3 tablespoons batter to each well, depending on the recipe. (The ice cream scoop holds 2 tablespoons).

3 Add the filling  If you are making filled pancakes, working quickly, carefully spoon about 1 teaspoon of the desired filling—here, raspberry jam—into the center of each pancake.

4 Enclose the filling  For filled pancakes, add about 1 tablespoon (half of a 1-ounce ice cream scoop) batter on top of the filling to enclose it. Cook the first side until bubbles rise from the centers of the pancakes and they are lightly browned and crisp on the bottom, 3–5 minutes.

5 Flip the pancakes  Position 2 short wooden skewers on opposite sides of a pancake, slide the tips between the edge of the well and the cooked edge, and lift and rotate gently. Repeat to turn the remaining pancakes.

6 Cook the second side  Cook the pancakes until lightly browned on the second side, about 3 minutes longer. Use the skewers to transfer the pancakes to a plate or platter.

# tips & tricks

You may need to cook a batch or two of ebelskivers before you feel comfortable making them. Once you're more accomplished, the following tips will help create perfect pancakes every time.

• Add the batter to the pan in an organized fashion: Start by spooning a portion into the centermost well. Next, add batter to the well at the 12:00 position. Work your way around the pan, filling the wells clockwise.

• Use the same clockwise pattern for filling and flipping that you started when adding batter to the pan, beginning with the center pancake. This will ensure evenly cooked ebelskivers.

• Look for small bubbles rising from the centers of the pancakes. This indicates that the ebelskivers are nearly ready to flip.

• When flipping the ebelskivers, don't worry if there is still liquid batter in the middle of the pancake. It will ooze into the bottom of the pan and, once cooked, will adhere to the rest of the pancake to form the characteristic sphere shape.

• After filling the pancakes, clean up any spills on the top of the pan with a damp paper towel, or scrape them away with a skewer, to ensure the ebelskivers release cleanly and stay intact.

• Be sure to let filled pancakes, especially those with fruit jam or similar fillings, cool slightly before eating to avoid burned mouths. Alert your guests or family members to the hot fillings inside the ebelskivers and encourage them to take care when eating.

**WORKING WITH EGGS**
Eggs are easiest to separate when cold, but the egg whites whip up better when they are at room temperature. If you have time, separate the eggs when chilled and then let the whites stand until room temperature, about 30 minutes, before beating.

# simple ebelskivers

# simple, but scrumptious

The recipes in this chapter start with basic, sugar-dusted ebelskivers and become increasingly more layered in flavor, from pancakes scented with cinnamon to treats studded with chocolate chips to puffs redolent with holiday spices.

Others are slicked with maple syrup, enriched with toasted coconut, infused with crunchy cornmeal, and served with fresh fruit compote. Many more tasty options are included to suit any mood or occasion.

# classic ebelskivers

Ebelskivers are amazingly versatile. The batter is forgiving; the ingredients can be simple or elaborate; and they can be served center stage or on the side. This classic sugar-dusted version is reminiscent of New Orleans–style beignets.

**Basic Batter, page 98**

**1 tablespoon unsalted butter, melted and slightly cooled**

**Confectioners' sugar for dusting**

Preheat the oven to 200°F (95°C). Make the batter as directed.

Brush the wells of the ebelskiver pan with some of the melted butter and place over medium heat. When the butter starts to bubble, add about 3 tablespoons batter to each well (see page 14).

Cook until the bottoms of the pancakes are lightly browned and crisp, 3–5 minutes. Use 2 short wooden skewers to turn all the pancakes (see page 14) and cook until lightly browned on the second side, about 3 minutes longer.

Transfer the finished pancakes to a platter and keep warm in the oven while you repeat to make 2 more batches. Dust the warm pancakes with the confectioners' sugar and serve right away.

Makes 21 pancakes; 4–7 servings

# crunchy cinnamon ebelskivers

These taste like cinnamon yeast rolls—but they're much easier to make. Brown sugar and butter are melted in the pan before the batter goes in. Once the cakes cool a little, the caramelized topping cracks brûlée-style with every bite.

Basic Batter, page 98

2 teaspoons ground cinnamon

¼ teaspoon freshly grated nutmeg

1 tablespoon unsalted butter, melted and slightly cooled

3½ tablespoons light brown sugar

Make the batter as directed, adding the cinnamon and nutmeg to the dry ingredients.

Brush the wells of the ebelskiver pan with some of the melted butter and place over medium heat. Working quickly, put ½ teaspoon of the brown sugar in each well and cook until the sugar melts and turns dark and syrupy, 3–5 minutes. Add about 3 tablespoons batter to each well (see page 14).

Cook until the bottoms of the pancakes are lightly browned and crisp, 3–5 minutes. Use 2 short wooden skewers to turn all the pancakes (see page 14) and cook until lightly browned on the second side, about 3 minutes longer.

Transfer the finished pancakes to a platter, let cool for 5 minutes, and serve slightly warm. Repeat to make 2 more batches, cooling each batch for 5 minutes before serving.

Makes 21 pancakes; 4–7 servings

# maple-nut ebelskivers

These nut-studded cakes are glossed with sweet, pure maple syrup. They're perfect for breakfast or as an unusual side dish with ham or pork. For an over-the-top dessert, serve them with Bourbon Whipped Cream (page 103).

1 cup (4 oz/120 g) pecans

Vanilla Batter, page 99

1/2 cup (4 fl oz/125 ml) pure maple syrup

1 tablespoon unsalted butter, melted and slightly cooled

Preheat the oven to 200°F (95°C). In a dry frying pan over medium heat, toast the pecans, stirring often, until lightly browned and fragrant, 3–5 minutes. Remove from the heat, transfer to a cutting board, and let cool slightly. Chop the pecans and set aside.

Make the batter as directed, adding half of the chopped nuts to the dry ingredients and 1/4 cup of the maple syrup to the wet ingredients.

Divide the remaining chopped pecans into 3 equal portions. Brush the wells of the ebelskiver pan with some of the melted butter and place over medium heat. Pour 1/2 teaspoon of the remaining maple syrup into each well. Working quickly, divide 1 portion of the pecans evenly among the wells. Cook until the syrup is bubbling, about 3 minutes. Add about 3 tablespoons batter to each well (see page 14).

Cook until the bottoms of the pancakes are lightly browned and crisp, 3–5 minutes. Use 2 short wooden skewers to turn all the pancakes (see page 14) and cook until lightly browned on the second side, about 3 minutes longer.

Transfer the finished pancakes to a platter and keep warm in the oven while you repeat to make 2 more batches. Serve right away.

Makes 21 pancakes; 4–7 servings

# chocolate chip ebelskivers

Making this recipe is even easier than whipping up a batch of chocolate chip cookies, and the results are just as satisfying. Typically the chips won't melt as they do in a cookie, but they do soften to an appealing creamy texture.

**Basic Batter, page 98**

**6 ounces (185 g) miniature semisweet chocolate chips**

**1 tablespoon unsalted butter, melted and slightly cooled**

Preheat the oven to 200°F (95°C). Make the batter as directed, folding in the chocolate chips with the last addition of egg whites.

Brush the wells of the ebelskiver pan with some of the melted butter and place over medium heat. When the butter starts to bubble, add about 3 tablespoons batter to each well (see page 14).

Cook until the bottoms of the pancakes are lightly browned and crisp, 3–5 minutes. Use 2 short wooden skewers to turn all the pancakes (see page 14) and cook until lightly browned on the second side, about 3 minutes longer.

Transfer the finished pancakes to a platter and keep warm in the oven while you repeat to make 2 more batches. Serve right away.

Makes 21 pancakes; 4–7 servings

# coconut ebelskivers

Toasted coconut gives the exterior of these cakes a classic golden-tipped crunch. Extra egg whites in the batter create a light, meringuelike interior reminiscent of coconut macaroons, with just half the preparation time.

½ cup (2½ oz/75 g) all-purpose flour

¼ teaspoon baking powder

¼ teaspoon salt

4 large eggs, separated

½ cup (4 fl oz/125 ml) whole milk

½ teaspoon pure vanilla extract

½ cup (2 oz/60 g) confectioners' sugar

1 cup (4 oz/120 g) sweetened shredded coconut

1 tablespoon unsalted butter, melted and slightly cooled

Preheat the oven to 200°F (95°C). In a large bowl, whisk together the flour, baking powder, and salt. Put 2 of the egg yolks in another bowl; reserve the remaining 2 yolks for another use. Add the milk and vanilla and whisk to blend. Add the yolk mixture to the flour mixture and, using a wooden spoon, stir until well blended. The batter will be lumpy.

In a clean bowl, beat the 4 egg whites until foamy. Slowly add the confectioners' sugar in 3 additions, beating well after each addition. Continue beating until the egg whites are glossy and stiff (see page 13), about 5 minutes. Using a rubber spatula, fold about one-third of the egg whites into the batter to lighten it, then fold in the rest together with ¾ cup of the coconut just until no white streaks remain.

Brush the wells of the ebelskiver pan with some of the melted butter and place over medium-low heat. When the butter starts to bubble, working quickly, spoon a heaping ½ teaspoon of the remaining coconut into each well. Add about 2 tablespoons batter to each well (see page 14). Cook until the bottoms of the pancakes are lightly browned and crisp, 5–7 minutes. Using 2 short wooden skewers, turn all the pancakes (see page 14) and cook until lightly browned on the second side, about 3 minutes longer.

Transfer the finished pancakes to a platter and keep warm in the oven while you repeat to make 2 more batches. Serve right away.

Makes 21 pancakes; 4–7 servings

# honey-glazed buttermilk ebelskivers

The spirit of the roadside diner lives in these light pancakes with the subtle tang of buttermilk and a sweet coating of honey. Dry buttermilk powder is a convenient way to keep buttermilk on hand; simply reconstitute it before use.

1 cup (5 oz/155 g)
all-purpose flour

1½ teaspoons sugar

1 teaspoon baking soda

½ teaspoon baking powder

¼ teaspoon freshly grated nutmeg

¼ teaspoon salt

2 large eggs, separated

1 cup (8 fl oz/250 ml) buttermilk

3 tablespoons unsalted butter, melted and slightly cooled

½ cup (6 oz/185 g) honey

Preheat the oven to 200°F (95°C). In a large bowl, whisk together the flour, sugar, baking soda, baking powder, nutmeg, and salt. In a small bowl, lightly whisk the egg yolks, then whisk in the buttermilk and 2 tablespoons of the melted butter. Add the yolk mixture to the flour mixture and, using a wooden spoon, stir until well blended. The batter will be lumpy.

In a clean bowl, beat the egg whites until stiff, but not dry, peaks form (see page 13). Using a rubber spatula, fold about one-third of the egg whites into the batter to lighten it, then fold in the rest just until no white streaks remain.

Brush the wells of the ebelskiver pan with some of the remaining melted butter and place over medium heat. Pour about 1 teaspoon of the honey into each well. When the honey starts to bubble, add about 2 tablespoons batter to each well (see page 14).

Cook until the bottoms of the pancakes are lightly browned and crisp, 3–5 minutes. Use 2 short wooden skewers to turn all the pancakes (see page 14) and cook until lightly browned on the second side, about 3 minutes longer.

Transfer the finished pancakes to a platter and keep warm in the oven while you repeat to make 2 more batches. Serve right away.

Makes 21 pancakes; 4–7 servings

# streusel-topped ebelskivers

In this recipe, all the best parts of a classic coffee cake, including butter and pecans, are cooked into the tops of the ebelskivers. Try tossing ½ cup of raspberries or blueberries into the topping for a burst of flavor and color.

**Pecan Streusel**

¼ **cup (1 oz/30 g) pecans**

¼ **cup (1½ oz/45 g) all-purpose flour**

¼ **cup (2 oz/60 g) firmly packed dark brown sugar**

**3 tablespoons unsalted butter, melted and slightly cooled**

**Basic Batter, page 98**

**1 teaspoon ground cinnamon**

**1 tablespoon unsalted butter, melted and slightly cooled**

**Confectioners' sugar for dusting**

To make the streusel, in a dry frying pan over medium heat, toast the pecans, stirring often, until lightly browned and fragrant, 3–5 minutes. Remove from the heat, transfer to a cutting board, and let cool slightly. Chop the pecans. In a small bowl, stir together the flour, brown sugar, melted butter, and chopped pecans. The mixture will be crumbly.

Preheat the oven to 200°F (95°C). Make the batter as directed, adding the cinnamon to the dry ingredients.

Brush the wells of the ebelskiver pan with some of the melted butter and place over medium heat. When the butter starts to bubble, working quickly, spoon about 1 teaspoon of the streusel into each well. Add about 2 tablespoons batter to each well (see page 14).

Cook until the bottoms of the pancakes are lightly browned and crisp, 3–5 minutes. Use 2 short wooden skewers to turn all the pancakes (see page 14) and cook until lightly browned on the other side, about 3 minutes longer.

Transfer the finished pancakes to a platter and keep warm in the oven while you repeat to make 2 more batches. Dust the warm pancakes with the confectioners' sugar and serve right away.

Makes 21 pancakes; 4–7 servings

# lemon–poppy seed ebelskivers

These pancakes are made with cake flour, giving them good structure and a muffinlike crumb. They make a great treat for school lunch boxes or picnic baskets, as, unlike many ebelskivers, they are good at room temperature.

1 cup (4 oz/125 g) cake flour

2 tablespoons granulated sugar

1/2 teaspoon baking powder

1/4 teaspoon salt

2 large eggs, separated

1 cup (8 fl oz/250 ml) whole milk

4 tablespoons (2 fl oz/60 ml) fresh lemon juice

Grated zest of 1 lemon

1 tablespoon poppy seeds

3 tablespoons unsalted butter, melted and slightly cooled

1/4 cup (1 oz/30 g) confectioners' sugar

Preheat the oven to 200°F (95°C). In a large bowl, whisk together the flour, granulated sugar, baking powder, and salt. In a small bowl, lightly whisk the egg yolks, then whisk in the milk, 2 tablespoons of the lemon juice, the lemon zest, poppy seeds, and 2 tablespoons of the melted butter. Add the yolk mixture to the flour mixture and, using a wooden spoon, stir until well blended. The batter will be lumpy.

In a clean bowl, beat the egg whites until stiff, but not dry, peaks form (see page 13). Using a rubber spatula, fold about one-third of the egg whites into the batter to lighten it, then fold in the rest just until no white streaks remain.

Brush the wells of the ebelskiver pan with some of the remaining melted butter and place over medium-low heat. When the butter starts to bubble, add about 2 1/2 tablespoons batter to each well (see page 14).

Cook until the bottoms of the pancakes are lightly browned and crisp, 3–5 minutes. Use 2 short wooden skewers to turn all the pancakes (see page 14) and cook until lightly browned on the second side, about 3 minutes longer.

Transfer the finished pancakes to a platter and repeat to make 2 more batches. In a bowl, blend the remaining 2 tablespoons lemon juice with the confectioners' sugar until smooth. Dip one side of the pancakes in the glaze or drizzle the glaze over the pancakes. Serve right away.

Makes 21 pancakes; 4–7 servings

# iced gingerbread ebelskivers

These frosted cakes are fun served on wooden sticks, lollipop style. Or, for kids, pile them on a platter with Orange Cream Ebelskivers (page 51) and Streusel-Topped Ebelskivers (page 31), and pipe faces on them with the glaze.

1 cup (5 oz/155 g) all-purpose flour

2 teaspoons ground ginger

1½ teaspoons granulated sugar

1 teaspoon ground cinnamon

½ teaspoon baking powder

¼ teaspoon freshly grated nutmeg

¼ teaspoon salt

2 large eggs, separated

1 cup (8 fl oz/250 ml) whole milk

½ cup (5½ oz/175 ml) dark molasses

3 tablespoons unsalted butter, melted and slightly cooled

1 cup (4 oz/125 g) confectioners' sugar

½ teaspoon pure vanilla extract

Preheat the oven to 200°F (95°C). In a large bowl, whisk together the flour, ginger, granulated sugar, cinnamon, baking powder, nutmeg, and salt. In a small bowl, lightly whisk the egg yolks, then whisk in the milk, molasses, and 2 tablespoons of the melted butter. Add the yolk mixture to the flour mixture and, using a wooden spoon, stir until well blended. The batter will be lumpy.

In a clean bowl, beat the egg whites until stiff, but not dry, peaks form (see page 13). Using a rubber spatula, fold about one-third of the egg whites into the batter to lighten it, then fold in the rest just until no white streaks remain.

Brush the wells of the ebelskiver pan with some of the remaining melted butter and place over medium heat. When the butter starts to bubble, add about 2 tablespoons batter to each well (see page 14).

Cook until the bottoms of the pancakes are lightly browned and crisp, 3–5 minutes. Use 2 short wooden skewers to turn all the pancakes (see page 14) and cook until lightly browned on the other side, about 3 minutes longer.

Transfer the finished pancakes to a platter and keep warm in the oven while you repeat to make 2 more batches. In a small bowl, stir together the confectioners' sugar, vanilla, and 2 teaspoons water until smooth. Drizzle the icing over the warm pancakes and serve right away.

Makes 21 pancakes; 4–7 servings

# corn cakes with blueberry compote

Sweet and nutty cornmeal pancakes are just as tasty alongside a bowl of chili as they are dressed with fruit or whipped cream. These ebelskivers, served with warm blueberry compote, are a fresh twist on a breakfast classic.

½ cup (2½ oz/75 g) all-purpose flour

½ cup (2½ oz/75 g) white cornmeal

1½ teaspoons granulated sugar

½ teaspoon baking powder

¼ teaspoon salt

2 large eggs, separated

1 cup (8 fl oz/250 ml) whole milk

3 tablespoons unsalted butter, melted and slightly cooled

Blueberry Compote, page 101

Preheat the oven to 200°F (95°C). In a large bowl, whisk together the flour, cornmeal, granulated sugar, baking powder, and salt. In small bowl, lightly whisk the egg yolks, then whisk in the milk and 2 tablespoons of the melted butter. Add the yolk mixture to the flour mixture and, using a wooden spoon, stir until well blended. The batter will be lumpy.

In a clean bowl, beat the egg whites until stiff, but not dry, peaks form (see page 13). Using a rubber spatula, fold about one-third of the egg whites into the batter to lighten it, then fold in the rest just until no white streaks remain.

Brush the wells of the ebelskiver pan with some of the remaining melted butter and place over medium heat. When the butter starts to bubble, add about 3 tablespoons batter to each well (see page 14).

Cook until the bottoms of the pancakes are lightly browned and crisp, 3–5 minutes. Use 2 short wooden skewers to turn all the pancakes (page 14) and cook until lightly browned on the second side, about 3 minutes longer.

Transfer the finished pancakes to a platter and keep warm in the oven while you repeat to make 2 more batches. Arrange the warm ebelskivers on individual plates and spoon the compote over the tops, or pass the compote in a bowl at the table. Serve right away.

Makes 21 pancakes; 4–7 servings

# sweet treats

# seriously sweet

This chapter shows how well ebelskivers lend themselves to a variety of fillings, from spiced apples to orange-scented cream cheese to chocolate ganache, yielding a surprise burst of flavor in each bite.

Sweet toppings, such as macerated strawberries, a sticky toffee mixture, or a chocolate dipping sauce, can also be added to dessert-style ebelskivers, on their own or in combination with the fillings, for an indulgent finale to a special dinner.

# cherry-almond ebelskivers

A combination of almond extract and ground toasted almonds lends deep notes of nutty flavor and a crunchy texture to these pancakes. Look for cherry preserves that have plump, whole cherries and a thick, syrupy jam.

**1 cup (4½ oz/140 g) slivered blanched almonds**

**Vanilla Batter, almond variation, page 99**

**1 tablespoon unsalted butter, melted and slightly cooled**

**½ cup (5 oz/155 g) good-quality cherry preserves**

Preheat the oven to 200°F (95°C). In a dry frying pan over medium heat, toast the almonds, stirring often, until lightly browned and fragrant, about 3 minutes. Transfer the nuts to a food processor, let cool slightly, and pulse just until coarse crumbs form. Be careful not to overprocess or the nuts will get buttery. Make the batter as directed, adding half of the ground almonds with the dry ingredients.

Brush the wells of the ebelskiver pan with some of the melted butter and place over medium heat. Divide the remaining ground almonds into 3 equal portions. Working with 1 portion, sprinkle half of the nuts evenly over the bottom and sides of the buttered wells. When the butter starts to bubble, add about 1 tablespoon batter to each well (see page 14). Working quickly, carefully spoon about 1 teaspoon of the cherry preserves into the center of each pancake. Top each with another 1 tablespoon batter. Sprinkle the tops with the remaining half-portion of ground nuts, dividing evenly.

Cook until the bottoms of the pancakes are lightly browned and crisp, 3–5 minutes. Use 2 short wooden skewers to turn all the pancakes (see page 14) and cook until lightly browned on the second side, about 3 minutes longer.

Transfer the finished pancakes to a platter and keep warm in the oven while you repeat to make 2 more batches. Serve warm.

Makes 21 pancakes; 4–7 servings

# double-blackberry ebelskivers

This recipe uses berries in two guises: as a surprising filling inside each pancake and as a sweet sauce poured over the top. For a smoother topping, push the warm berries through a sieve and drizzle on the finished pancakes.

2 cups (8 oz/250 g) fresh blackberries

1–2 tablespoons sugar

Vanilla Batter, page 99

1 tablespoon unsalted butter, melted and slightly cooled

Set aside 21 blackberries for the pancakes. Add the remaining berries to a nonreactive saucepan with sugar to taste. Warm over medium heat, stirring occasionally, until the berries have burst and the juices are rendered, about 5 minutes. Set the blackberry sauce aside.

Preheat the oven to 200°F (95°C). Make the batter as directed.

Brush the wells of the ebelskiver pan with some of the melted butter and place over medium heat. When the butter starts to bubble, add about 1 tablespoon batter to each well (see page 14). Working quickly, place a whole blackberry in the center of each pancake. Top each with another 1 tablespoon batter.

Cook until the bottoms of the pancakes are lightly browned and crisp, 3–5 minutes. Use 2 short wooden skewers to turn all the pancakes (see page 14) and cook until lightly browned on the second side, about 3 minutes longer.

Transfer the finished pancakes to a platter and keep warm in the oven while you repeat to make 2 more batches. Serve right away with the blackberry sauce.

Makes 21 pancakes; 4–7 servings

# raspberry jam–filled ebelskivers

As these pancakes cook, the jam inside oozes through the cracks in the batter, then caramelizes on the outsides, making them both crisp and syrupy at the same time. The seeds in the jam lend an appealing, crunchy texture.

**Basic Batter, page 98**

**1 tablespoon unsalted butter, melted and slightly cooled**

**½ cup (5 oz/155 g) raspberry jam, with seeds or seedless**

Preheat the oven to 200°F (95°C). Make the batter as directed.

Brush the wells of the ebelskiver pan with some of the melted butter and place over medium heat. When the butter starts to bubble, add about 1 tablespoon batter to each well (see page 14). Working quickly, carefully spoon about 1 teaspoon of the raspberry jam into the center of each pancake. Top each with another 1 tablespoon batter.

Cook until the bottoms of the pancakes are lightly browned and crisp, 3–5 minutes. Use 2 short wooden skewers to turn all the pancakes (see page 14) and cook until lightly browned on the second side, about 3 minutes longer.

Transfer the finished pancakes to a platter and keep warm in the oven while you repeat to make 2 more batches. Serve right away.

Makes 21 pancakes; 4–7 servings

# jelly donut ebelskivers

For pancakes with gooey stripes of color and flavor cooked right into the crust, stir a little additional jelly into the batter, leaving broad streaks, before filling the cups. For added crunch, use demerara sugar instead of superfine.

**Vanilla Batter, page 99**

**1 tablespoon unsalted butter, melted and slightly cooled**

**1/2 cup (5 oz/155 g) strawberry or grape jelly, or your favorite jam or preserves**

**3 teaspoons superfine sugar**

Preheat the oven to 200°F (95°C). Make the batter as directed.

Brush the wells of the ebelskiver pan with some of the melted butter and place over medium heat. When the butter starts to bubble, add about 1 tablespoon batter to each well (see page 14). Working quickly, carefully spoon about 1 teaspoon of the jelly into the center of each pancake. Top each with another 1 tablespoon batter.

Cook until the bottoms of the pancakes are lightly browned and crisp, 3–5 minutes. Use 2 short wooden skewers to turn all the pancakes (see page 14) and cook until lightly browned on the second side, about 3 minutes longer.

Transfer the finished pancakes to a platter and keep warm in the oven while you repeat to make 2 more batches. Sprinkle the sugar over the warm pancakes and serve right away.

Makes 21 pancakes; 4–7 servings

# ebelskivers with spiced apple filling

In Denmark, ebelskivers are served at markets, community gatherings, and in homes during the winter holidays. This recipe with spiced apple filling invokes the traditional pancakes from which all ebelskiver recipes are derived.

**Spiced Apple Filling**

¼ cup (2 oz/60 g) unsalted butter

3 tablespoons granulated sugar

¼ teaspoon ground cinnamon

¼ teaspoon freshly grated nutmeg

Pinch of salt

2 tart green apples such as Granny Smith, peeled, cored, and diced

Vanilla Batter, page 99

1 tablespoon unsalted butter, melted and slightly cooled

Confectioners' sugar for dusting

To make the filling, in a saucepan over medium-high heat, melt the butter. Add the sugar, cinnamon, nutmeg, and salt and cook, stirring to dissolve the sugar, just until bubbly, 3–5 minutes. Add the apples, reduce the heat to medium, and cook, stirring often, until the apples are tender, about 10 minutes. Remove from the heat and set aside.

Preheat the oven to 200°F (95°C). Make the batter as directed.

Brush the wells of the ebelskiver pan with some of the melted butter and place over medium heat. When the butter starts to bubble, add about 1 tablespoon batter to each well (see page 14). Working quickly, carefully spoon about 1 teaspoon of the apple filling into the center of each pancake. Top each with another 1 tablespoon batter.

Cook until the bottoms of the pancakes are lightly browned and crisp, 3–5 minutes. Use 2 short wooden skewers to turn all the pancakes (see page 14) and cook until lightly browned on the second side, about 3 minutes longer.

Transfer the finished pancakes to a platter and keep warm in the oven while you repeat to make 2 more batches. Dust the warm ebelskivers with confectioners' sugar and serve right away.

Makes 21 pancakes; 4–7 servings

# banana-rum pancakes

Reminiscent of bananas Foster, these pancakes make a New Orleans–style finale to a festive dinner. Try these the next time you are trying to impress your guests with your culinary skills—they'll never guess how easy they are to make.

**Banana Filling**

**2 ripe bananas, chopped**

**¼ cup (2 oz/60 g) firmly packed light brown sugar**

**¼ teaspoon freshly grated nutmeg**

**Pinch of salt**

**2 tablespoons unsalted butter**

**Vanilla Batter, page 99**

**1 tablespoon unsalted butter, melted and slightly cooled**

**Rum Sauce, page 101**

**Vanilla Whipped Cream, page 103**

To make the filling, in a bowl, toss the bananas with the brown sugar, nutmeg, and salt until well coated. In a sauté pan, melt the butter over medium heat. Stir in the banana mixture and cook until the bananas are softened and the liquid is syrupy, 5–7 minutes. Remove from the heat and set aside.

Preheat the oven to 200°F (95°C). Make the batter as directed.

Brush the wells of the ebelskiver pan with some of the melted butter and place over medium heat. When the butter starts to bubble, add about 1 tablespoon batter to each well (see page 14). Working quickly, carefully spoon about 1 teaspoon of the banana filling into the center of each pancake. Top each with another 1 tablespoon batter.

Cook until the bottoms of the pancakes are lightly browned and crisp, 3–5 minutes. Use 2 short wooden skewers to turn all the pancakes (see page 14) and cook until lightly browned on the second side, about 3 minutes longer.

Transfer the finished pancakes to a platter and keep warm in the oven while you repeat to make 2 more batches. Arrange the warm pancakes on individual plates, spoon the rum sauce over the tops, and top with whipped cream. Serve right away.

Makes 21 pancakes; 4–7 servings

# orange cream ebelskivers

Better than oatmeal and not nearly the work of waffles, these pancakes go well with any breakfast menu. For a delicious dessert, fold a splash of orange liqueur into the cream filling and drizzle the pancakes with flavored honey.

**½ cup (6 oz/185 g) whipped-style cream cheese**

**Grated zest of 1 orange**

**1 teaspoon confectioners' sugar, plus more for dusting**

**Orange Batter, page 100**

**1 tablespoon unsalted butter, melted and slightly cooled**

In a bowl, blend the cream cheese with the orange zest and 1 teaspoon confectioners' sugar until smooth. Cover and refrigerate until needed.

Preheat the oven to 200°F (95°C). Make the batter as directed.

Brush the wells of the ebelskiver pan with some of the melted butter and place over medium heat. When the butter starts to bubble, add about 1 tablespoon batter to each well (see page 14). Working quickly, carefully spoon about 1 teaspoon of the cream cheese mixture into the center of each pancake. Top each with another 1 tablespoon batter.

Cook until the bottoms of the pancakes are lightly browned and crisp, 3–5 minutes. Use 2 short wooden skewers to turn all the pancakes (see page 14) and cook until lightly browned on the second side, about 3 minutes longer.

Transfer the finished pancakes to a platter and keep warm in the oven while you repeat to make 2 more batches. Dust the warm ebelskivers with confectioners' sugar and serve right away.

Makes 21 pancakes; 4–7 servings

# lemon curd–filled ebelskivers

Arrange these tangy pancakes on a platter with Orange Cream Ebelskivers (page 51), garnished with whipped cream and orange zest. You'll have more curd than you need, but it freezes well. Or, use about ½ cup purchased lemon curd.

### Lemon Curd

**Juice of 2 lemons**

**6 tablespoons (3 oz/ 90 g) granulated sugar**

**2 large eggs, plus 3 egg yolks**

**¼ cup (2 oz/60 g) unsalted butter**

**Basic Batter, page 98**

**1 tablespoon grated lemon zest**

**1 tablespoon unsalted butter, melted and slightly cooled**

**Confectioners' sugar for dusting**

To make the lemon curd, in a large heatproof bowl, combine the lemon juice, sugar, eggs, yolks, and butter. Place in a saucepan over (not touching) gently simmering water. Cook, whisking constantly, until the butter melts. Continue to cook, stirring with a wooden spoon, until the mixture coats the back of the spoon, about 3 minutes; do not let it boil. Strain through a fine-mesh sieve into a bowl. Press plastic wrap directly on the surface and refrigerate until well chilled, about 3 hours.

Preheat the oven to 200°F (95°C). Make the batter as directed, adding the lemon zest with the wet ingredients.

Brush the wells of the ebelskiver pan with some of the melted butter and place over medium heat. When the butter starts to bubble, add about 1 tablespoon batter to each well (see page 14). Working quickly, carefully spoon about 1 teaspoon of the lemon curd into the center of each pancake. Top each with another 1 tablespoon batter.

Cook until the bottoms of the pancakes are lightly browned and crisp, 3–5 minutes. Use 2 short wooden skewers to turn all the pancakes (see page 14) and cook until lightly browned on the second side, about 3 minutes longer.

Transfer the finished pancakes to a platter and keep warm in the oven while you repeat to make 2 more batches. Dust the warm ebelskivers with confectioners' sugar and serve right away.

Makes 21 pancakes; 4–7 servings

# strawberry shortcake pancakes

Here, strawberries are macerated in sugar, rendering the juices to make a sweet, colorful glaze (for a little kick, add a splash of kirsch). Poured over the pancakes and layered with whipped cream, it becomes an indulgent treat.

1 pint (8 oz/250 g) strawberries, hulled and sliced

3 teaspoons sugar

Vanilla Batter, page 99

½ teaspoon freshly grated nutmeg

1 tablespoon unsalted butter, melted and slightly cooled

Vanilla Whipped Cream, page 103

Preheat the oven to 200°F (95°C). In a bowl, toss the strawberries with the granulated sugar and set aside. Make the batter as directed, adding the nutmeg with the dry ingredients.

Brush the wells of the ebelskiver pan with some of the melted butter and place over medium heat. When the butter starts to bubble, add about 3 tablespoons batter to each well (see page 14).

Cook until the bottoms of the pancakes are lightly browned and crisp, 3–5 minutes. Use 2 short wooden skewers to turn all the pancakes (see page 14) and cook until lightly browned on the other side, about 3 minutes longer.

Transfer the finished pancakes to a platter and keep warm in the oven while you repeat to make 2 more batches. Arrange the warm ebelskivers in wide, individual bowls. Spoon some strawberries with their syrup alongside, top with the whipped cream, and serve right away.

Makes 21 pancakes; 4–7 servings

# cream cheese–filled spiced pancakes

These pancakes, scented with cinnamon and nutmeg and with a delicious creamy filling and sweet crust, are a bundle of perfect pleasures for breakfast. Serve with strong, hot coffee in place of a traditional Danish or roll.

½ cup (6 oz/185 g) whipped-style cream cheese, at room temperature

3 teaspoons confectioners' sugar

½ teaspoon vanilla extract

Vanilla Batter, page 99

2 teaspoons ground cinnamon

¼ teaspoon freshly grated nutmeg

1 tablespoon unsalted butter, melted and slightly cooled

Preheat the oven to 200°F (95°C). In a bowl, using a rubber spatula, blend the cream cheese with 1 teaspoon of the confectioners' sugar and the vanilla until smooth. Set aside. Make the batter as directed, adding 1 teaspoon of the cinnamon and the nutmeg with the dry ingredients.

Brush the wells of the ebelskiver pan with some of the melted butter and place over medium heat. When the butter starts to bubble, add about 1 tablespoon batter to each well (see page 14). Working quickly, carefully spoon about 1 teaspoon of the cream cheese filling into the center of each pancake. Top each with another 1 tablespoon batter.

Cook until the bottoms of the pancakes are lightly browned and crisp, 3–5 minutes. Use 2 short wooden skewers to turn all the pancakes (see page 14) and cook until lightly browned on the second side, about 3 minutes longer.

Transfer the finished pancakes to a platter and keep warm in the oven while you repeat to make 2 more batches. In a small bowl, sift together the remaining 2 teaspoons confectioners' sugar and the remaining 1 teaspoon cinnamon. Dust the warm pancakes with the cinnamon-sugar mixture and serve right away.

Makes 21 pancakes; 4–7 servings

# peanut butter & jelly ebelskivers

Lovers of the classic PB&J sandwich, especially kids, will swoon for this stuffed version. The peanutty batter is delicious with a variety of fillings in place of jam, from butterscotch chips to chocolate sauce to mini marshmallows.

1 cup (5 oz/155 g) all-purpose flour

1½ teaspoons sugar

½ teaspoon baking powder

¼ teaspoon salt

2 large eggs, separated

1 cup (8 fl oz/250 ml) whole milk

½ cup (5 oz/155 g) creamy peanut butter

3 tablespoons unsalted butter, melted and slightly cooled

½ cup (5 oz/155 g) grape jelly, strawberry jam, or your favorite preserves or jam

Preheat the oven to 200°F (95°C). In a large bowl, whisk together the flour, sugar, baking powder, and salt. In a small bowl, lightly whisk the egg yolks, then whisk in the milk, peanut butter, and 2 tablespoons of the melted butter until smooth. Add the yolk mixture to the flour mixture and, using a wooden spoon, stir until well blended. The batter will be lumpy.

In a clean bowl, beat the egg whites until stiff, but not dry, peaks form (see page 13). Fold about one-third of the egg whites into the batter to lighten it, then fold in the rest just until no white streaks remain.

Brush the wells of the ebelskiver pan with some of the remaining melted butter and place over medium heat. When the butter starts to bubble, add about 1 tablespoon batter to each well (see page 14). Working quickly, carefully spoon about 1 teaspoon of the jelly into the center of each pancake. Top each with another 1 tablespoon batter.

Cook until the bottoms of the pancakes are lightly browned and crisp, 3–5 minutes. Use 2 short wooden skewers to turn all the pancakes (see page 14) and cook until lightly browned on the second side, about 3 minutes longer.

Transfer the finished pancakes to a platter and keep warm in the oven while you repeat to make 2 more batches. Serve right away.

Makes 21 pancakes; 4–7 servings

# sticky toffee ebelskivers

This indulgent recipe is a take on a classic British dessert. The pancakes are filled with a rum-spiked date filling, and then topped with an unctuous toffee-flavored sauce. Top them with whipped cream for an over-the-top dessert.

Date Filling

½ **cup (3 oz/90 g) dried dates**

½ **teaspoon pure vanilla extract**

¼ **teaspoon dark rum**

3 **tablespoons firmly packed dark brown sugar**

½ **teaspoon baking soda**

⅛ **teaspoon salt**

⅓ **cup (3 fl oz/80 ml) boiling water**

½ **cup (2 oz/60 g) chopped toasted pecans**

Basic Batter, page 98

1 **tablespoon unsalted butter, melted and slightly cooled**

Sticky Toffee Sauce, page 102

To make the filling, in a large heatproof bowl, combine the dates, vanilla, rum, sugar, baking soda, and salt. Pour the boiling water over the top and let stand until the dates are rehydrated, the sugar is dissolved, and the mixture has cooled slightly, about 15 minutes. Purée the mixture in a food processor until smooth. Stir in the chopped pecans and set aside.

Preheat the oven to 200°F (95°C). Make the batter as directed.

Brush the wells of the ebelskiver pan with some of the melted butter and place over medium heat. When the butter starts to bubble, add about 1 tablespoon batter to each well (see page 14). Working quickly, carefully spoon about 1 teaspoon of the date filling into the center of each pancake. Top with another 1 tablespoon batter.

Cook until the bottoms of the pancakes are lightly browned and crisp, 3–5 minutes. Use 2 short wooden skewers to turn all the pancakes (see page 14) and cook until lightly browned on the second side, about 3 minutes longer.

Transfer the finished pancakes to a platter and keep warm in the oven while you repeat to make 2 more batches. Spoon a small amount of toffee sauce into wide individual bowls and arrange the warm ebelskivers on top. Spoon a little more of the toffee sauce over the tops and serve right away.

Makes 21 ebelskivers; 4–7 servings

# chocolate truffle ebelskivers

A simple ganache can be used for everything from cake icing to truffles, or as a gooey filling for fluffy pancakes. For a grand dessert, serve these *profiterole*-style with Dark Chocolate Sauce, page 102 and Vanilla Whipped Cream, page 103.

Chocolate Ganache

**6 ounces (185 g) semisweet chocolate, chopped**

**1 cup (8 fl oz/250 ml) heavy cream**

**Basic Batter, page 98**

**1 tablespoon unsalted butter, melted and slightly cooled**

To make the ganache, place the chocolate in a heatproof bowl. In a saucepan, warm the cream over medium heat just until small bubbles form around the edges of the pan. Do not let it boil. Pour the hot cream over the chocolate and stir until well blended and smooth. Set aside and let cool. Once cool, refrigerate until well chilled, at least 1 hour or preferably overnight.

Preheat the oven to 200°F (95°C). Prepare the batter as directed.

Brush the wells of the ebelskiver pan with some of the melted butter and place over medium heat. When the butter starts to bubble, add about 1 tablespoon batter to each well (see page 14). Working quickly, carefully spoon about ½ teaspoon of the ganache into the center of each pancake. Top with another 1 tablespoon batter. Reserve the remaining ganache for another use.

Cook until the bottoms of the pancakes are lightly browned and crisp, 3–5 minutes. Use 2 short wooden skewers to turn all the pancakes (see page 14) and cook until lightly browned on the second side, about 3 minutes longer.

Transfer the finished pancakes to a platter and keep warm in the oven while you repeat to make 2 more batches. Serve right away.

Makes 21 pancakes; 4–7 servings

# pumpkin pie ebelskivers

To make a creamy filling for these cakes, blend ½ cup whipped cream cheese with ½ teaspoon vanilla extract. To double the richness, make a little extra, sweeten it with a tablespoon of superfine sugar, and use it as a frosting.

½ cup (1½ oz/45 g) graham cracker crumbs (see page 104)

¼ cup (1½ oz/45 g) all-purpose flour

¼ cup (2 oz/60 g) firmly packed light brown sugar

1 tablespoon pumpkin pie spice

½ teaspoon baking powder

¼ teaspoon salt

2 large eggs, separated

1 can (14 oz/440 g) sweetened condensed milk

3 tablespoons unsalted butter, melted and slightly cooled

1 can (15 oz/470 g) pumpkin purée

Confectioners' sugar for dusting

Preheat the oven to 200°F (95°C). In a large bowl, whisk together the graham cracker crumbs, flour, brown sugar, pumpkin pie spice, baking powder, and salt. In a small bowl, lightly whisk the egg yolks, then whisk in the condensed milk and 2 tablespoons of the melted butter. Add the yolk mixture to the flour mixture and, using a wooden spoon, stir until well blended. The batter will be lumpy.

In a clean bowl, beat the egg whites until stiff, but not dry, peaks form (see page 13). Fold the egg whites into the batter alternately with the pumpkin purée in 2 additions, just until well blended and no white streaks remain.

Brush the wells of the ebelskiver pan with some of the melted butter and place over medium heat. When the butter starts to bubble, add about 2 tablespoons batter to each well (see page 14).

Cook until the bottoms of the pancakes are lightly browned and crisp, 3–5 minutes. Use 2 short wooden skewers to turn all the pancakes (see page 14) and cook until lightly browned on the other side, about 3 minutes longer.

Transfer the finished pancakes to a platter and keep warm in the oven while you repeat to make 2 more batches. Dust the warm ebelskivers with confectioners' sugar and serve right away.

Makes 21 pancakes; 4–7 servings

# ebelskivers, s'mores style

Here, ebelskivers evoke the campground with the addition of graham cracker crumbs to the batter, giving the finished pancakes a terrific crunch. Add a teaspoon of instant espresso to the dipping sauce for a sophisticated flavor.

½ cup (1½ oz/45 g) all-purpose flour

½ cup (1½ oz/45 g) graham cracker crumbs (see page 104)

1½ teaspoons sugar

½ teaspoon baking powder

¼ teaspoon freshly grated nutmeg

¼ teaspoon salt

2 large eggs, separated

1 cup (8 fl oz/250 ml) whole milk

3 tablespoons unsalted butter, melted and slightly cooled

½ cup (1 oz/30 g) marshmallow crème

Chocolate Dipping Sauce, page 102

Preheat the oven to 200°F (95°C). In a large bowl, whisk together the flour, cracker crumbs, sugar, baking powder, nutmeg, and salt. In a bowl, lightly whisk the egg yolks, then whisk in the milk and 2 tablespoons of the melted butter. Add the yolk mixture to the flour mixture and, using a wooden spoon, stir until well blended. The batter will be lumpy.

In a clean bowl, beat the egg whites until stiff, but not dry, peaks form (see page 13). Fold about one-third of the egg whites into the batter to lighten it, then fold in the rest just until no white streaks remain.

Brush the wells of the ebelskiver pan with some of the remaining melted butter and place over medium heat. When the butter starts to bubble, add about 1 tablespoon batter to each well (see page 14). Using 2 teaspoons dipped in cold water, carefully spoon about 1 teaspoon of the marshmallow crème into the center of each pancake. Top each with another 1 tablespoon batter.

Cook until the bottoms of the pancakes are lightly browned and crisp, 3–5 minutes. Use 2 short wooden skewers to turn all the pancakes (see page 14) and cook until lightly browned on the other side, about 3 minutes longer.

Transfer the finished pancakes to a platter and keep warm in the oven while you repeat to make 2 more batches. Serve right away, drizzled with the chocolate sauce.

Makes 21 pancakes; 4–7 servings

# salted caramel–pecan ebelskivers

With a crisp shell and buttery caramel filling, these pancakes taste like a cross between a coffee cake and a candy bar. For a simple and elegant garnish, dust the finished pancakes with confectioners' sugar instead of the salt.

1 cup (4 oz/120 g) pecans

Vanilla Batter, page 99

1 tablespoon unsalted butter, melted and slightly cooled

½ cup (4 fl oz/125 ml) Caramel Sauce (page 103) or good-quality purchased caramel dessert topping, plus more for drizzling, optional

Large-flake sea salt, such as Maldon

Preheat the oven to 200°F (95°C). In a dry frying pan over medium heat, toast the pecans, stirring often, until lightly browned and fragrant, 3–5 minutes. Transfer to a food processor and let cool slightly. Pulse just until coarse crumbs form. Be careful not to overprocess or the nuts will get buttery. Make the batter as directed, adding the chopped pecans with the dry ingredients.

Brush the wells of the ebelskiver pan with some of the melted butter and place over medium heat. When the butter starts to bubble, add about 1 tablespoon batter to each well (see page 14). Working quickly, carefully spoon about 1 teaspoon of the caramel sauce into the center of each pancake. Top each with another 1 tablespoon batter.

Cook until the bottoms of the pancakes are lightly browned and crisp, 3–5 minutes. Use 2 short wooden skewers to turn all the pancakes (see page 14) and cook until lightly browned on the other side, about 3 minutes longer.

Transfer the finished pancakes to a platter and keep warm in the oven while you repeat to make 2 more batches. If desired, drizzle the warm pancakes with additional caramel sauce. Sprinkle with a pinch or two of salt and serve right away.

Makes 21 pancakes; 4–7 servings

# molten chocolate ebelskivers

Intensely rich, these ebelskivers can be served a few at a time with sweetened whipped cream. For something more dramatic, sprinkle servings with chocolate shavings, best-quality cocoa powder, or confectioners' sugar.

**12 ounces (375 g) bittersweet chocolate, coarsely chopped**

**Vanilla Batter, page 99**

**1 tablespoon unsalted butter, melted and slightly cooled**

Place the chocolate in the top pan of a double boiler or a heatproof bowl and place over, but not touching, a pan of boiling water. Stir the chocolate until melted and smooth. Remove from the heat and set aside to cool.

Preheat the oven to 200°F (95°C). Make the batter as directed, adding half of the cooled melted chocolate with the wet ingredients.

Brush the wells of the ebelskiver pan with some of the melted butter and place over medium heat. When the butter starts to bubble, add about 1 tablespoon batter to each well (see page 14). Working quickly, carefully spoon about 1 teaspoon of the melted chocolate into the center of each pancake. Top each with another 1 tablespoon batter.

Cook until the bottoms of the pancakes are lightly browned and crisp, 3–5 minutes. Use 2 short wooden skewers to turn all the pancakes (see page 14) and cook until lightly browned on the second side, about 3 minutes longer.

Transfer the finished pancakes to a platter and keep warm in the oven while you repeat to make 2 more batches. Serve right away.

Makes 21 pancakes; 4–7 servings

# savory snacks

# savory & satisfying

The novel shape and ease of preparation make ebelskivers infinitely versatile. This chapter offers recipes for snacks, hors d'oeuvres, appetizers, or even unusual side dishes in the classic ebelskiver form.

Many are riffs on popular dishes, such as potato pancakes, crab cakes, and spinach and feta turnovers. Cheese, vegetables, poultry, cured meats, and seafood all make tasty additions to these tiny treats.

# herb & goat cheese ebelskivers

These tangy pancakes are delicious served with anything from a crisp white wine to a brothy vegetable soup. If you prefer, mix 2½ tablespoons of chopped fresh sage or another herb into the batter instead of using the leaves.

Basic Batter, page 98

1 tablespoon unsalted butter, melted and slightly cooled

21 small fresh sage leaves

3½ tablespoons chilled and crumbled goat cheese

Preheat the oven to 200°F (95°C). Make the batter as directed.

Brush the wells of the ebelskiver pan with some of the melted butter and place over medium heat. When the butter starts to bubble, carefully place 1 sage leaf on the bottom of each well, then add about 1 tablespoon batter (see page 14). Working quickly, carefully spoon about ½ teaspoon of the goat cheese into the center of each pancake. Top each with another 1 tablespoon batter.

Cook until the bottoms of the pancakes are lightly browned and crisp, 3–5 minutes. Use 2 short wooden skewers to turn all the pancakes (see page 14) and cook until lightly browned on the second side, about 3 minutes longer.

Transfer the finished pancakes to a platter and keep warm in the oven while you repeat to make 2 more batches. Serve right away.

Makes 21 pancakes; 4–7 servings

# ebelskiver popovers

Using an ovenproof ebelskiver pan with a metal handle, you can make tiny popovers with moist, hollow centers and beautifully irregular, puffed, and crusty golden tops. They are best served hot, slathered in fresh butter.

1 tablespoon plus
1 teaspoon unsalted
butter, melted and
slightly cooled

1 cup (5 oz/155 g)
all-purpose flour

1 cup (8 fl oz/250 ml)
whole milk

2 large eggs

1½ teaspoons
kosher salt

In a blender or food processor, combine the 1 tablespoon melted butter, the flour, milk, eggs, and salt and process until well blended and smooth, about 30 seconds. Transfer the batter to a bowl and let rest in the refrigerator for at least 30 minutes or up to 2 hours.

Place an ebelskiver pan on the center oven rack and preheat the oven to 400°F (200°C). Let the pan heat in the oven for 10–15 minutes.

Using oven mitts, carefully remove the hot pan from the oven. Working quickly, brush the pan's wells with some of the remaining melted butter. Fill each well about three-fourths full with the batter, taking care not to overfill the wells.

Return the pan to the oven and bake until the tops are fully puffed and golden brown, about 20 minutes. Do not open the oven during the baking time or the popovers may not rise correctly.

Turn the popovers out onto a wire rack, cover with a clean kitchen towel, and repeat with the remaining batter to make a second batch. Serve the popovers warm.

Makes 14 mini popovers; 4–6 servings

# walnut, pear & blue cheese pancakes

These ebelskivers wrap their golden pancake crust around a popular combination of flavors. For an even bolder flavor, use a ripe Gorgonzola. Toasting the walnuts mellows their bitterness and gives them crunch.

1 cup (5 oz/155 g)
all-purpose flour

1/2 teaspoon sugar

1/2 teaspoon baking
powder

1/4 teaspoon salt

2 large eggs, separated

1 cup (8 fl oz/250 ml)
whole milk

3 tablespoons unsalted
butter, melted and
slightly cooled

Pear Compote,
page 101

1/4 cup (1 oz/30 g)
walnuts, toasted and
chopped

1/4 cup (1 1/2 oz/40 g)
crumbled blue cheese

Preheat the oven to 200°F (95°C). In a large bowl, whisk together the flour, sugar, baking powder, and salt. In a small bowl, lightly whisk the egg yolks, then whisk in the milk and 2 tablespoons of the melted butter. Add the yolk mixture to the flour mixture and, using a wooden spoon, stir until well blended. The batter will be lumpy.

In a clean bowl, beat the egg whites until stiff, but not dry, peaks form (see page 13). Fold about one-third of the egg whites into the batter to lighten it, then fold in the rest just until no white streaks remain.

Brush the wells of the ebelskiver pan with some of the remaining melted butter and place over medium heat. When the butter starts to bubble, add about 1 tablespoon batter to each well (see page 14). Working quickly, carefully spoon a heaping 1/2 teaspoon each of the pear compote, walnuts, and blue cheese into the center of each pancake. Top each with another 1 tablespoon batter.

Cook until the bottoms of the pancakes are lightly browned and crisp, 3–5 minutes. Use 2 short wooden skewers to turn all the pancakes (see page 14) and cook until lightly browned on the second side, about 3 minutes longer.

Transfer the finished pancakes to a platter and keep warm in the oven while you repeat to make 2 more batches. Serve right away.

Makes 21 pancakes; 4–7 servings

# miniature stove-top cheese soufflés

These light pancakes with a cheesy bite are cousins to the *petits soufflés* served in small ramekins in French bistros. They have all of the impact but none of the intimidation raised by the image of a tall, golden-capped soufflé.

1 cup (5 oz/155 g) all-purpose flour

1 teaspoon sugar

1/2 teaspoon baking powder

1/4 teaspoon salt

2 large eggs, separated, plus 2 large egg whites

1 cup (8 fl oz/250 ml) whole milk

3 tablespoons unsalted butter, melted and slightly cooled

1 cup (4 oz/125 g) shredded Gruyère cheese

1/4 teaspoon freshly ground pepper

Preheat the oven to 200°F (95°C). In a large bowl, whisk together the flour, sugar, baking powder, and salt. In a small bowl, lightly whisk the 2 egg yolks, then whisk in the milk and 2 tablespoons of the melted butter. Add the yolk mixture to the flour mixture and, using a wooden spoon, stir until well blended. The batter will be lumpy.

In a clean bowl, beat the 4 egg whites until stiff, but not dry, peaks form (see page 13). Fold the egg whites and the cheese into the batter in 3 additions, until no white streaks remain.

Brush the wells of the ebelskiver pan with some of the remaining melted butter and place over medium heat. When the butter starts to bubble, working quickly, sprinkle a pinch of pepper into each well. Add about 2 tablespoons batter to each well (see page 14).

Cook until the bottoms of the pancakes are lightly browned and crisp, 3–5 minutes. Use 2 short wooden skewers to turn all the pancakes (see page 14) and cook until lightly browned on the second side, about 3 minutes longer.

Transfer the finished pancakes to a platter and keep warm in the oven while you repeat to make 2 more batches. Serve right away.

Makes 21 pancakes; 4–7 servings

# spicy corn ebelskivers

These pancakes are the perfect accompaniment for chili or Mexican-style soup. They're great served with a piquant green salsa and salty margaritas. Fill these with a little *queso fresco* as they cook for a cooling contrast to the chiles.

½ cup (2½ oz/75 g) each all-purpose flour and white cornmeal

1½ teaspoons sugar

¾ teaspoon baking powder

¼ teaspoon salt

2 large eggs, separated

1 cup (8 fl oz/250 ml) whole milk

3 tablespoons unsalted butter, melted and slightly cooled

4 green onions, finely chopped

1 jalapeño chile, stemmed and seeded, finely chopped

1½ cups (6 oz/90 g) shredded Monterey jack cheese

1 cup (6 oz/185 g) fresh corn kernels or thawed frozen corn, coarsely chopped

Tomatillo Salsa, page 104, or 2 cups (16 fl oz/500 ml) purchased salsa

Preheat the oven to 200°F (95°C). In a large bowl, whisk together the flour, cornmeal, sugar, baking powder, and salt. Set aside. In a small bowl, lightly whisk the egg yolks, then whisk in the milk and 2 tablespoons of the melted butter. Add the yolk mixture to the flour mixture and, using a wooden spoon, stir until well blended. The batter will be lumpy.

In a clean bowl, beat the egg whites until stiff, but not dry, peaks form (see page 13). Fold about one-third of the egg whites into the batter to lighten it, then fold in the rest just until no white streaks remain. Gently fold in the green onions, jalapeño, cheese, and corn kernels, taking care not to deflate the mixture.

Brush the wells of the ebelskiver pan with some of the remaining melted butter and place over medium heat. When the butter starts to bubble, add about 2 tablespoons batter to each well (see page 14).

Cook until the bottoms of the pancakes are lightly browned and crisp, 3–5 minutes. Use 2 short wooden skewers to turn all the pancakes (see page 14) and cook until lightly browned on the second side, about 3 minutes longer.

Transfer the finished pancakes to a platter and keep warm in the oven while you repeat to make 2 more batches. Serve right away with the tomatillo salsa.

Makes 21 pancakes; 4–7 servings

# potato & green onion pancakes

These versatile pancakes are just as tasty topped with caviar as they are with ketchup. Butter or sour cream are also nice accompaniments. Serve as a snack or as an interesting companion to roasted or grilled meats.

**2–3 medium russet potatoes, peeled and shredded, or 3 cups (15 oz/470 g) thawed frozen shredded potatoes**

**½ cup (2½ oz/75 g) all-purpose flour**

**½ teaspoon sugar**

**½ teaspoon baking powder**

**¼ teaspoon salt**

**¼ teaspoon freshly ground pepper**

**2 large eggs, separated**

**1 cup (8 fl oz/250 ml) whole milk**

**3 tablespoons unsalted butter, melted and slightly cooled**

**6 green onions, white and tender green parts, finely chopped**

Preheat the oven to 200°F (95°C). Place the shredded potatoes between layers of paper towels and squeeze to soak up most of the moisture. Set aside. In a large bowl, whisk together the flour, sugar, baking powder, salt, and pepper. In a small bowl, lightly whisk the egg yolks, then whisk in the milk and 2 tablespoons of the melted butter. Add the yolk mixture to the flour mixture and, using a wooden spoon, stir until well blended. The batter will be lumpy.

In a clean bowl, using an electric mixer, beat the egg whites until stiff, but not dry, peaks form (see page 13). Fold about one-third of the egg whites into the batter to lighten it, then fold in the rest just until no white streaks remain. Gently fold in the potatoes and green onions, taking care not to deflate the mixture.

Brush the wells of the ebelskiver pan with some of the remaining melted butter and place over medium heat. When the butter starts to bubble, add about 2 tablespoons batter to each well (see page 14).

Cook until the bottoms of the pancakes are lightly browned and crisp, 3–5 minutes. Use 2 short wooden skewers to turn all the pancakes (see page 14) and cook until lightly browned on the second side, about 3 minutes longer.

Transfer the finished pancakes to a platter and keep warm in the oven while you repeat to make 2 more batches. Serve right away.

*Makes 21 pancakes; 4–7 servings*

# mushroom & pancetta ebelskivers

A handful of fresh thyme adds herbal brightness to the batter and complements the mushrooms in these ebelskivers. For a vegetarian version, rehydrate a few dried morel mushrooms and use in place of the pancetta.

**1 cup (5 oz/155 g) all-purpose flour**

**2½ tablespoons chopped fresh thyme**

**½ teaspoon baking powder**

**¼ teaspoon salt**

**2 large eggs, separated**

**1 cup (8 fl oz/250 ml) whole milk**

**3 tablespoons unsalted butter, melted and slightly cooled**

**Mushroom & Pancetta Ragout, page 104**

Preheat the oven to 200°F (95°C). In a large bowl, whisk together the flour, thyme, baking powder, and salt. Set aside. In a small bowl, lightly whisk the egg yolks, then whisk in the milk and 2 tablespoons of the melted butter. Add the yolk mixture to the flour mixture and, using a wooden spoon, stir until well blended. The batter will be lumpy.

In a clean bowl, beat the egg whites until stiff, but not dry, peaks form (see page 13). Fold about one-third of the egg whites into the batter to lighten it, then fold in the rest just until no white streaks remain.

Brush the wells of the ebelskiver pan with some of the remaining butter and place over medium heat. When the butter starts to bubble, add about 1 tablespoon batter to each well (see page 14). Working quickly, carefully spoon 1 teaspoon of the mushroom and pancetta ragout into the center of each pancake. Top with another 1 tablespoon batter.

Cook until the bottoms of the pancakes are lightly browned and crisp, 3–5 minutes. Use 2 short wooden skewers to turn all the pancakes (see page 14) and cook until lightly browned on the second side, about 3 minutes longer.

Transfer the finished pancakes to a platter and keep warm in the oven while you repeat to make 2 more batches. Serve right away.

Makes 21 pancakes; 4–7 servings

# spinach & feta pancakes

These pancakes make great appetizers with cocktails or partners to a main-course salad. Other cooking greens, like chard or kale, can be used in place of the spinach. Be sure to remove the stems and large veins from the greens.

**10 ounces (315 g) frozen chopped spinach, thawed**

**1 cup (4 oz/125 g) cake flour**

**2 1/2 teaspoons minced fresh oregano, or 1 teaspoon dried**

**1/2 teaspoon sugar**

**1/2 teaspoon baking powder**

**1/4 teaspoon salt**

**2 large eggs, separated**

**1 cup (8 fl oz/250 ml) whole milk**

**3 tablespoons unsalted butter, melted and slightly cooled**

**1/2 cup (2 1/2 oz/80 g) crumbled feta cheese**

Preheat the oven to 200°F (95°C). Drain the spinach thoroughly. In a large bowl, whisk together the flour, oregano, sugar, baking powder, and salt. In a small bowl, lightly whisk the egg yolks, then whisk in the milk and 2 tablespoons of the melted butter. Add the yolk mixture and the spinach to the flour mixture and, using a wooden spoon, stir until well blended. The batter will be lumpy.

In a clean bowl, beat the egg whites until stiff, but not dry, peaks form (see page 13). Fold about one-third of the egg whites into the batter to lighten it, then fold in the rest just until no white streaks remain.

Brush the wells of the ebelskiver pan with some of the remaining melted butter and place over medium heat. When the butter starts to bubble, add about 1 tablespoon batter to each well (see page 14). Working quickly, carefully spoon 1 rounded teaspoon of the feta into the center of each pancake. Top with another 1 tablespoon batter.

Cook until the bottoms of the pancakes are lightly browned and crisp, 3–5 minutes. Use 2 short wooden skewers to turn all the pancakes (see page 14) and cook until lightly browned on the second side, about 3 minutes longer.

Transfer the finished pancakes to a platter and keep warm in the oven while you repeat to make 2 more batches. Serve right away.

Makes 21 pancakes; 4–7 servings

# ebelskivers, crab cake style

Make these cakes when crab is in season so you can take advantage of the bounty of fresh, sweet crabmeat at your local fish market. When fresh is not available, high-quality canned crab, rinsed well and drained, will do nicely.

1 cup (4 oz/125 g) cake flour

2 teaspoons Old Bay seasoning

1 teaspoon baking powder

1/4 teaspoon salt

2 large eggs, separated

1 cup (8 fl oz/250 ml) whole milk

3 tablespoons unsalted butter, melted and slightly cooled

5 ounces (155 g) fresh lump crabmeat, picked over for cartilage and shell fragments

1 celery stalk, finely chopped

1 small shallot, minced

2 1/2 tablespoons chopped fresh flat-leaf (Italian) parsley

1/4 teaspoon Worcestershire sauce

Red Pepper Aioli, page 104

Preheat the oven to 200°F (95°C). In a large bowl, whisk together the flour, Old Bay seasoning, baking powder, and salt. In a small bowl, lightly whisk the egg yolks, then whisk in the milk and 2 tablespoons of the melted butter. Add the yolk mixture to the flour mixture and, using a wooden spoon, stir until well blended. The batter will be lumpy.

In a clean bowl, beat the egg whites until stiff, but not dry, peaks form (see page 13). Fold about one-third of the egg whites into the batter to lighten it, then fold in the rest just until no white streaks remain. Gently fold in the crabmeat, celery, shallot, parsley, and Worcestershire, taking care not to deflate the mixture.

Brush the wells of the ebelskiver pan with some of the remaining butter and place over medium heat. When the butter starts to bubble, add about 3 tablespoons batter to each well (see page 14).

Cook until the bottoms of the pancakes are lightly browned and crisp, 3–5 minutes. Using 2 short wooden skewers, turn all the pancakes (see page 14) and cook until lightly browned on the second side, about 3 minutes longer.

Transfer the finished pancakes to a platter and keep warm in the oven while you repeat to make 2 more batches. Serve right away with the red pepper aioli.

Makes 21 pancakes; 4–7 servings

# tomato-stuffed polenta cakes

While the distinctive ingredients here are from Italian cuisine, don't be tempted to brush the pan with olive oil instead of butter; the oil will produce a heavy, soggy, crust while butter ensures consistently crisp exteriors.

½ cup (2½ oz/75 g) all-purpose flour

½ cup (2½ oz/75 g) quick-cooking polenta

¼ cup freshly grated Parmesan cheese

1½ teaspoons sugar

½ teaspoon baking powder

½ teaspoon freshly ground pepper

¼ teaspoon salt

2 large eggs, separated

1 cup (8 fl oz/250 ml) whole milk

3 tablespoons unsalted butter, melted and slightly cooled

3½ tablespoons sun-dried tomato purée

Preheat the oven to 200°F (95°C). In a large bowl, whisk together the flour, polenta, Parmesan, sugar, baking powder, pepper, and salt. Set aside. In a small bowl, lightly whisk the egg yolks, then whisk in the milk and 2 tablespoons of the melted butter. Add the yolk mixture to the flour mixture and, using a wooden spoon, stir until well blended. The batter will be lumpy.

In a clean bowl, beat the egg whites until stiff, but not dry, peaks form (see page 13). Fold about one-third of the egg whites into the batter to lighten it, then fold in the rest just until no white streaks remain.

Brush the wells of the ebelskiver pan with some of the remaining melted butter and place over medium heat. When the butter starts to bubble, add about 1 tablespoon batter to each well (see page 14). Working quickly, carefully spoon about ½ teaspoon of the tomato purée into the center of each pancake. Top each with another 1 tablespoon batter.

Cook until the bottoms of the pancakes are lightly browned and crisp, 3–5 minutes. Use 2 short wooden skewers to turn all the pancakes (see page 14), and cook until lightly browned on the second side, about 3 minutes longer.

Transfer the finished pancakes to a platter and keep warm in the oven while you repeat to make 2 more batches. Serve right away.

Makes 21 pancakes; 4–7 servings

# chicken bites with creamy dressing

Serve this easy, stove-top version of fried chicken croquettes with hot soup for a great kid-friendly lunch or supper. The homemade ranch-style dressing is made special with tangy Parmesan cheese and fresh herbs.

1 cup (5 oz/155 g) all-purpose flour

½ teaspoon baking powder

¼ teaspoon salt

¼ teaspoon freshly ground pepper

2 large eggs, separated

1 cup (8 fl oz/250 ml) whole milk

3 tablespoons unsalted butter, melted and slightly cooled

4 ounces (125 g) chopped cooked chicken breast meat

2½ tablespoons chopped fresh flat-leaf (Italian) parsley

1 shallot, finely chopped

Buttermilk Dressing, page 105

Preheat the oven to 200°F (95°C). In a large bowl, whisk together the flour, baking powder, salt, and pepper. In a small bowl, lightly whisk the egg yolks, then whisk in the milk and 2 tablespoons of the melted butter. Add the yolk mixture to the flour mixture and, using a wooden spoon, stir until well blended. The batter will be lumpy.

In a clean bowl, beat the egg whites until stiff, but not dry, peaks form (see page 13). Fold about one-third of the egg whites into the batter to lighten it, then fold in the rest just until no white streaks remain. Gently fold in the chicken, parsley, and shallot, taking care not to deflate the mixture.

Brush the wells of the ebelskiver pan with some of the remaining melted butter and place over medium heat. When the butter starts to bubble, add about 2 tablespoons of the batter to each well (page 14).

Cook until the bottoms of the pancakes are lightly browned and crisp, 3–5 minutes. Use 2 short wooden skewers to turn all the pancakes (see page 14) and cook until lightly browned on the other side, about 3 minutes longer.

Transfer the finished pancakes to a platter and keep warm in the oven while you repeat to make 2 more batches. Serve right away with the buttermilk dressing for dipping.

Makes 21 pancakes; 4–7 servings

# smoked salmon & dill ebelskivers

These pancakes showcase the classic combination of salmon, cream cheese, and tangy fresh dill and make a welcome addition to a Sunday brunch buffet. They're also perfect as a warm hors d'oeuvre at a cocktail party.

Basic Batter, page 98

1/2 teaspoon freshly ground pepper

1 teaspoon fresh lemon juice

1/4 cup (1/3 oz/10 g) firmly packed chopped fresh dill

1 tablespoon unsalted butter, melted and slightly cooled

3 1/2 tablespoons minced smoked salmon (about 4 oz/125 g)

3 1/2 tablespoons whipped-style cream cheese, at room temperature

Preheat the oven to 200°F (95°C). Make the batter as directed, adding the pepper with the dry ingredients and the lemon juice with the liquid ingredients. Stir the dill into the finished batter.

Brush the wells of the ebelskiver pan with some of the melted butter and place over medium heat. When the butter starts to bubble, add about 1 tablespoon batter to each well (see page 14). Working quickly, carefully spoon about 1/2 teaspoon of the smoked salmon into the center of each pancake, then spoon about 1/2 teaspoon of the cream cheese on top. Top each with another 1 tablespoon batter.

Cook until the bottoms of the pancakes are lightly browned and crisp, 3–5 minutes. Use 2 short wooden skewers to turn all the pancakes (see page 14) and cook until lightly browned on the second side, about 3 minutes longer.

Transfer the finished pancakes to a platter and keep warm in the oven while you repeat to make 2 more batches. Serve right away.

Makes 21 pancakes; 4–7 servings

# fig & prosciutto ebelskivers

Fresh figs are not in season for long, but good-quality fig jam makes a delicious substitute. To use fresh figs here, chop 5 or 6 figs and cook over medium heat with 1 tablespoon each butter and brown sugar until tender.

1 cup (5 oz/155 g) all-purpose flour

1/2 teaspoon sugar

1/2 teaspoon baking powder

1/4 teaspoon salt

2 large eggs, separated

1 cup (8 fl oz/250 ml) whole milk

3 tablespoons unsalted butter, melted and slightly cooled

3 1/2 tablespoons fig jam

3 1/2 tablespoons finely chopped prosciutto, sautéed until crisp

Preheat the oven to 200°F (95°C). In a large bowl, whisk together the flour, sugar, baking powder, and salt. In a small bowl, lightly whisk the egg yolks, then whisk in the milk and 2 tablespoons of the melted butter. Add the yolk mixture to the flour mixture and, using a wooden spoon, stir until well blended. The batter will be lumpy.

In a clean bowl, beat the egg whites until stiff, but not dry, peaks form (see page 13). Fold about one-third of the egg whites into the batter to lighten it, then fold in the rest just until no white streaks remain.

Brush the wells of the ebelskiver pan with some of the remaining melted butter and place over medium heat. When the butter starts to bubble, add about 1 tablespoon batter to each well (see page 14). Working quickly, carefully spoon 1/2 teaspoon of the jam into the center of each pancake, then place 1/2 teaspoon of the prosciutto on top. Top each with another 1 tablespoon batter.

Cook until the bottoms of the pancakes are lightly browned and crisp, 3–5 minutes. Use 2 short wooden skewers to turn all the pancakes (see page 14) and cook until lightly browned on the second side, about 3 minutes longer.

Transfer the finished pancakes to a platter and keep warm in the oven while you repeat to make 2 more batches. Serve right away.

Makes 21 pancakes; 4–7 servings

# two-cheese puffs with marinara

These savory dough balls, stuffed with two types of Italian cheese and dipped in zesty marinara sauce, are reminiscent of miniature calzones. Making them—and then eating them—is a great activity to try with kids on a rainy afternoon.

1 cup (4 oz/125 g) cake flour

3/4 teaspoon baking powder

1/4 teaspoon salt

2 large eggs, separated

1 cup (8 fl oz/250 ml) whole milk

3 tablespoons unsalted butter, melted and slightly cooled

1/2 cup (2 oz/60 g) freshly grated Parmesan cheese

2 1/2 tablespoons chopped fresh basil

3 1/2 tablespoons finely diced fresh mozzarella

1 cup (8 fl oz/250 ml) Marinara Sauce (page 105) or purchased marinara sauce

Preheat the oven to 200°F (95°C). In a large bowl, whisk together the flour, baking powder, and salt. In a small bowl, lightly whisk the egg yolks, then whisk in the milk and 2 tablespoons of the melted butter. Add the yolk mixture to the flour mixture and, using a wooden spoon, stir until well blended. The batter will be lumpy.

In a clean bowl, beat the egg whites until stiff, but not dry, peaks form (see page 13). Fold about one-third of the egg whites into the batter to lighten it, then fold in the rest with 1/4 cup of the Parmesan and the basil just until no white streaks remain.

Brush the wells of the ebelskiver pan with some of the remaining melted butter and place over medium heat. When the butter starts to bubble, working quickly, sprinkle a heaping 1/2 teaspoon of the remaining Parmesan into each well. Add about 1 tablespoon batter into each well (see page 14), then carefully add 1/2 teaspoon mozzarella to the center of each pancake. Top each with another 1 tablespoon batter.

Cook until the bottoms of the pancakes are lightly browned and crisp, 3–5 minutes. Use 2 short wooden skewers to turn all the pancakes (see page 14) and cook until lightly browned on the second side, about 3 minutes longer.

Transfer the finished pancakes to a platter and keep warm in the oven while you repeat to make 2 more batches. Serve with the marinara.

Makes 21 puffs; 4–7 servings

# batters, etc.

## a wealth of tasty choices

This chapter contains three staple batters: one all-purpose recipe, one vanilla-infused option, and one orange-flavored mixture, all of which will inspire endless creativity.

Also featured here are a variety of sweet and savory fillings, toppings, and accompaniments to serve with your pancakes, adding plenty of flavor to and inspiration for the tiny treats.

# basic batter

This is a workhorse batter, perfect for sweet and savory ebelskivers alike. The small amount of sugar mixed with the dry ingredients helps the pancakes brown and both enhances sweet flavorings and offsets savory ingredients.

1 cup (5 oz/155 g) all-purpose flour

1½ teaspoons sugar

½ teaspoon baking powder

¼ teaspoon salt

2 large eggs, separated

1 cup (8 fl oz/250 ml) whole milk

2 tablespoons unsalted butter, melted and slightly cooled

In a large bowl, whisk together the flour, sugar, baking powder, and salt. In a small bowl, lightly whisk the egg yolks, then whisk in the milk and melted butter. Add the yolk mixture to the flour mixture and, using a wooden spoon, stir until well blended. The batter will be lumpy.

In a clean bowl, using an electric mixer on high speed, beat the egg whites until stiff, but not dry, peaks form (see page 13). Using a silicone spatula, fold about one-third of the egg whites into the batter to lighten it, then fold in the rest just until no white streaks remain. Use the batter right away.

Makes batter for 21 pancakes

# vanilla batter

Scented with pure vanilla extract, this batter is perfect for a variety of breakfast- or dessert-style ebelskivers. To turn this into almond batter, as in Cherry-Almond Ebelskivers, page 43, substitute almond extract for vanilla.

1 cup (5 oz/155 g) all-purpose flour

1½ teaspoons sugar

½ teaspoon baking powder

¼ teaspoon salt

2 large eggs, separated

1 cup (8 fl oz/250 ml) whole milk

2 tablespoons unsalted butter, melted and slightly cooled

½ teaspoon pure vanilla extract

In a large bowl, whisk together the flour, sugar, baking powder, and salt. In a small bowl, lightly whisk the egg yolks, then whisk in the milk, melted butter, and vanilla extract. Add the yolk mixture to the flour mixture and, using a wooden spoon, stir until well blended. The batter will be lumpy.

In a clean bowl, using an electric mixer on high speed, beat the egg whites until stiff, but not dry, peaks form (see page 13). Using a rubber spatula, fold about one-third of the egg whites into the batter to lighten it, then fold in the rest just until no white streaks remain. Use the batter right away.

Makes batter for 21 pancakes

# orange batter

This batter uses cake flour in place of all-purpose flour, lending the pancakes a finer, cakelike texture and additional loft. The addition of orange juice in place of half of the usual milk gives the finished ebelskivers a fresh citrus taste.

1 cup (4 oz/125 g)
cake flour

1½ teaspoons sugar

½ teaspoon baking
powder

¼ teaspoon salt

2 large eggs, separated

½ cup (4 fl oz/125 ml)
whole milk

½ cup (4 fl oz/125 ml)
fresh orange juice

2 tablespoons unsalted
butter, melted and
slightly cooled

In a large bowl, whisk together the flour, sugar, baking powder, and salt. In a small bowl, lightly whisk the egg yolks, then whisk in the milk, orange juice, and melted butter. Add the yolk mixture to the flour mixture and, using a wooden spoon, stir until well blended. The batter will be lumpy.

In a clean bowl, using an electric mixer on high speed, beat the egg whites until stiff, but not dry, peaks form (see page 13). Using a rubber spatula, fold about one-third of the egg whites into the batter to lighten it, then fold in the rest just until no white streaks remain. Use the batter right away.

Makes batter for 21 pancakes

# fillings, toppings & sauces

The following recipes can enhance a variety of different ebelskivers, whether served morning, noon, or night. Versatile fillings, toppings, and dipping sauces are offered, as well as a recipe for homemade graham cracker crumbs.

## Blueberry Compote

**3 cups (12 oz/375 g) fresh blueberries or 12 ounces (375 g) thawed frozen blueberries, with their liquid**

**2 tablespoons light brown sugar**

**1/4 teaspoon freshly grated nutmeg**

**1/4 teaspoon pure vanilla extract**

In a saucepan over medium-high heat, combine the blueberries, 2–3 tablespoons water (if using fresh berries), the sugar, nutmeg, and vanilla. Cook, stirring often, until the berries have burst and released their juices, and the mixture is bubbly and slightly thickened, about 5 minutes. Remove from the heat and set aside to cool slightly before using as a filling or topping.

Makes about 3 cups (24 fl oz/750 ml)

## Pear Compote

**1 tablespoon unsalted butter**

**1 tablespoon light brown sugar**

**1 small Bartlett pear, peeled, cored, and cut into 1/4-inch (6 mm) dice**

In a small saucepan over medium heat, melt the butter. Add the brown sugar and diced pear and cook, stirring occasionally, until the fruit is softened and the liquid is syrupy, 7–10 minutes. Remove from the heat, let cool, and use as needed for a filling or topping.

Makes about 1/2 cup (4 fl oz/125 ml)

## Rum Sauce

**1/2 teaspoon cornstarch**

**1/2 cup (4 oz/125 g) sugar**

**1/2 cup (4 fl oz/125 ml) dark rum**

**1/2 teaspoon pure vanilla extract**

**1 tablespoon unsalted butter**

In a saucepan over medium heat, dissolve the cornstarch in 1/2 cup (4 fl oz/125 ml) water. Add the sugar and cook, stirring often, until the mixture is bubbling, about 5 minutes. Add the rum and vanilla, then stir in the butter. Cook, stirring occasionally, until the mixture has thickened slightly, about 5 minutes. Let cool to room temperature before using.

Makes about 3/4 cup (6 fl oz/180 ml)

## Sticky Toffee Sauce

5 tablespoons (2½ oz/75 g) unsalted butter

¾ cup (6 oz/185 g) firmly packed dark brown sugar

⅛ teaspoon salt

½ cup (4 fl oz/125 ml) heavy cream

2 teaspoons dark rum

In a small saucepan over medium heat, melt the butter. Add the sugar, 2 tablespoons water, and the salt and bring the mixture to a simmer. Cook, stirring occasionally, until the sugar is completely dissolved and the liquid thickens slightly, about 8 minutes. Remove from the heat and whisk in the cream and rum until smooth. Return the pan to medium-low heat and cook, stirring occasionally, until the sauce is the consistency of thick syrup, 8–10 minutes more.

Makes about ¾ cup (6 fl oz/180 ml)

## Chocolate Dipping Sauce

½ cup (4 oz/125 g) sugar

⅔ cup (2 oz/60 g) unsweetened cocoa powder, preferably Dutch process

¼ teaspoon salt

1 teaspoon pure vanilla extract

In a saucepan, combine ¾ cup (6 fl oz/180 ml) water and the sugar. Bring to a boil over high heat and cook, stirring often, until the sugar is dissolved and the mixture is clear, 3–5 minutes. Whisk in the cocoa powder and salt, reduce the heat to medium, and simmer until the mixture is smooth and slightly thickened, about 3 minutes longer. Remove from the heat and stir in the vanilla. The sauce will thicken a little more as it cools. (The sauce can be made up to 3 days in advance and stored, tightly covered, in the refrigerator.)

Makes about ¾ cup (6 fl oz/180 ml)

## Dark Chocolate Sauce

¾ cup (6 oz/185 g) unsalted butter, cut into small pieces

2 oz (60 g) unsweetened chocolate, chopped

¼ cup (¾ oz/20 g) unsweetened cocoa powder, preferably Dutch process

1 cup (8 oz/250 g) sugar

Pinch of salt

1 cup (8 fl oz/250 ml) heavy cream

1 teaspoon pure vanilla extract

In a saucepan over low heat, slowly melt the butter and chocolate, stirring occasionally, until smooth. Remove from the heat.

In a small bowl, stir together the cocoa powder, sugar, and salt. Add to the chocolate mixture and stir to combine. Add the cream, raise the heat to medium-low, and heat gently until smooth and warm. Remove from the heat and stir in the vanilla. The sauce will thicken as it cools. (The sauce can be made up to 3 days in advance and stored, tightly covered, in the refrigerator. Reheat gently over low heat before using.)

Makes about 2 cups (16 fl oz/500 ml)

## Caramel Sauce

1½ cups (12 oz/375 g) sugar
1¼ cups (10 fl oz/315 ml) heavy cream
Pinch salt

In a heavy, high-sided saucepan, cook the sugar over medium-high heat until it begins to melt around the edges, about 5 minutes. Continue to cook, stirring with a wooden spoon, until the sugar is melted and turns medium amber in color, about 3 minutes.

Protecting your hands and arms with oven mitts, very carefully pour the cream down the sides of the pan in a slow, steady steam (it will bubble and spatter violently), stirring constantly until completely smooth. Stir in the salt. Transfer the mixture to a small heatproof bowl and let cool completely.

If using the sauce as a filling, cover and refrigerate the mixture until firm, about 2 hours. To use as a sauce, reheat the mixture gently over low heat until smooth and warm. (The sauce can be made up to 3 days in advance and stored, tightly covered in the

refrigerator. Use straight from the refrigerator as a filling. Reheat gently over low heat before using as a sauce.)

Makes about 2½ cups (20 fl oz/625 ml)

## Vanilla Whipped Cream

1 cup (8 fl oz/250 ml) heavy cream
1 teaspoon pure vanilla extract
2 tablespoons confectioners' sugar

In a large bowl, combine the cream and vanilla extract. Using an electric mixer on high speed, beat the mixture until foamy. While beating continuously, slowly add the confectioners' sugar and beat until soft peaks form. Cover and refrigerate until ready to use.

Makes about 1½ cups (12 fl oz/375 ml)

## Bourbon Whipped Cream

1 cup (8 fl oz/250 ml) heavy cream
2 tablespoons bourbon whisky
1 teaspoon sugar

In a large bowl, combine the cream and bourbon. Using an electric mixer on high speed, beat the mixture until foamy. While beating continuously, slowly add the sugar and beat until soft peaks form. Cover and refrigerate until ready to use.

Makes about 1½ cups (12 fl oz/375 ml)

## Graham Cracker Crumbs

**3 full-size graham crackers**

Put the graham crackers in a zippered plastic bag and seal well. Using a rolling pin, crush the crackers until they are reduced to fine crumbs. Alternatively, pulse the crackers in a food processor until fine crumbs form.

Makes about ½ cup (4 fl oz/125 ml)

## Tomatillo Salsa

**1½ pounds (24 oz/750 g) tomatillos, husks and stems removed, and rinsed well**

**¼ cup (¼ oz/8 g) firmly packed fresh cilantro leaves**

**1 jalapeño chile, stemmed and seeded**

**2 tablespoons fresh lime juice**

**¼ teaspoon salt**

**¼ teaspoon sugar**

Preheat the broiler. Coarsely chop the tomatillos, then spread in a single layer in a roasting pan. Place the pan under the broiler and broil just until the tomatillos soften and their color intensifies, about 5 minutes. Transfer to a bowl and set aside to cool. Place the cooled tomatillos in a food processor and add the cilantro, jalapeño, lime juice, salt, and sugar. Pulse until well blended but still chunky. Taste and adjust the seasonings. Transfer the salsa to a small bowl, cover, and refrigerate until ready to serve. Bring to room temperature before serving. (The salsa will keep, covered in the refrigerator, for up to 3 days.)

Makes about 3 cups (24 fl oz/750 ml)

## Mushroom & Pancetta Ragout

**4 ounces (125 g) assorted wild mushrooms**

**1 tablespoon extra-virgin olive oil**

**2 garlic cloves, chopped**

**4 ounces (90 g) pancetta, finely diced**

**½ cup (4 fl oz/125 ml) heavy cream**

Brush clean the mushrooms, remove and discard any tough stems, and then finely chop. In a large frying pan, heat the olive oil over medium heat. Add the garlic and pancetta and cook, stirring often, until the pancetta starts to brown, about 5 minutes. Add the mushrooms and cook, stirring occasionally, until the mushrooms have given off their juices, softened, and browned. Stir in the cream and simmer until slightly thickened, about 5 minutes. Let cool slightly before using.

Makes about ½ cup (4 fl oz/125 ml)

## Red Pepper Aioli

**1 red bell pepper**

**2 large egg yolks**

**2 tablespoons fresh lemon juice**

**1 garlic clove**

**1 teaspoon capers**

³/₄ cup (6 fl oz/180 ml) extra-virgin olive oil
Salt and freshly ground pepper to taste

Preheat the broiler. Place the pepper directly on the oven rack 4–6 inches from the heat source and broil, turning often, until the skin is blistered on all sides. Transfer to a paper bag, seal the bag, set aside. When cool enough to handle, peel the blackened skin from the pepper, then remove the stem and seeds. Place the pepper in a food processor and process to a smooth purée. Transfer to a large bowl.

Thoroughly wash and dry the food processor work bowl. In the food processor, combine the egg yolks, lemon juice, garlic, and capers and process until smooth. With the motor running, slowly pour the oil through the feed tube in a slow, steady stream and process until the mixture has thickened, 3–5 minutes. Transfer the aioli to the bowl with the pepper purée and, using a rubber spatula, blend the mixtures until no red streaks remain. Season to taste with salt and pepper. Cover and refrigerate until ready to serve. (The aioli will keep, tightly covered in the refrigerator, for up to 2 days.) Note: If you're short on time, blend the red pepper purée with ³/₄ cup (6 fl oz/180 ml) high-quality mayonnaise.

Makes about 1 cup (8 fl oz/250 ml)

## Buttermilk Dressing

³/₄ cup (6 fl oz/180 ml) best-quality mayonnaise
¹/₄ cup (2 fl oz/60 ml) buttermilk
2¹/₂ tablespoons chopped fresh flat-leaf parsley
2 tablespoons freshly grated Parmesan cheese
1 teaspoon dried minced onion
Salt and freshly ground pepper to taste

In a bowl, whisk together the mayonnaise, buttermilk, parsley, cheese, and dried onion until blended. Season to taste with salt and pepper. Cover and refrigerate for at least 2 hours, or up to 8 hours, to blend the flavors.

Makes about 1 cup (8 fl oz/250 ml)

## Marinara Sauce

2 cloves garlic, minced
¹/₄ cup extra-virgin olive oil
Pinch red pepper flakes
1 teaspoon *each* dried basil and oregano
1 can (15 oz/410 g) crushed Italian tomatoes
Salt and freshly ground pepper to taste

In a large frying pan over medium heat, sauté the garlic in the olive oil until fragrant, about 1 minute. Stir in the red pepper flakes, basil, oregano, and tomatoes and bring to a simmer. Reduce the heat to low and simmer until thickened, about 20 minutes. Season to taste.

Makes about 2¹/₂ cups (20 fl oz/625 ml)

# serving ebelskivers

In Denmark, ebelskivers are traditionally served as a sweet snack. But thanks to the wide variety of recipes in this book, and as the following ideas show, these small pancakes can be served nearly any time of the day.

## for appetizers

Herb & Goat Cheese Ebelskivers

•

Walnut, Pear & Blue Cheese Pancakes

•

Miniature Stove-Top Cheese Soufflés

•

Spicy Corn Ebelskivers

•

Potato & Green Onion Pancakes

•

Mushroom & Pancetta Ebelskivers

•

Spinach & Feta Ebelskivers

•

Ebelskivers, Crab Cake Style

•

Tomato-Stuffed Polenta Cakes

•

Chicken Bites with Creamy Dressing

•

Smoked Salmon & Dill Ebelskivers

•

Fig & Prosciutto Ebelskivers

•

Two-Cheese Puffs with Marinara

## for snacks or side dishes

Classic Ebelskivers

•

Crunchy Cinnamon Ebelskivers

•

Chocolate Chip Ebelskivers

•

Coconut Ebelskivers

•

Streusel-Topped Ebelskivers

•

Lemon-Poppy Seed Ebelskivers

•

Herb & Goat Cheese Ebelskivers

•

Ebelskiver Popovers

•

Spicy Corn Ebelskivers

•

Potato & Green Onion Pancakes

•

Mushroom & Pancetta Ebelskivers

•

Spinach & Feta Ebelskivers

•

Tomato-Stuffed Polenta Cakes

•

Chicken Bites with Creamy Dressing

•

Two-Cheese Puffs with Marinara

## for breakfast or brunch

Classic Ebelskivers

•

Crunchy Cinnamon Ebelskivers

•

Maple-Nut Ebelskivers

•

Chocolate Chip Ebelskivers

•

Honey-Glazed Buttermilk
Ebelskivers

•

Streusel-Topped Ebelskivers

•

Lemon-Poppy Seed Ebelskivers

•

Corn Cakes with Blueberry Compote

•

Cherry-Almond Ebelskivers

•

Double-Blackberry Ebelskivers

•

Raspberry Jam–Filled Ebelskivers

•

Jelly Donut Ebelskivers

•

Ebelskivers with Spiced Apple Filling

•

Orange Cream Ebelskivers

•

Lemon Curd–Filled Ebelskivers

•

Cream Cheese–Filled
Spiced Pancakes

•

Miniature Stove-Top Cheese
Soufflés

•

Potato & Green Onion Pancakes

•

Smoked Salmon & Dill Ebelskivers

## for dessert

Crunchy Cinnamon Ebelskivers

•

Maple-Nut Ebelskivers

•

Chocolate Chip Ebelskivers

•

Coconut Ebelskivers

•

Lemon-Poppy Seed Ebelskivers

•

Iced Gingerbread Ebelskivers

•

Cherry-Almond Ebelskivers

•

Double-Blackberry Ebelskivers

•

Raspberry Jam–Filled Ebelskivers

•

Ebelskivers with Spiced Apple Filling

•

Banana-Rum Pancakes

•

Orange Cream Ebelskivers

•

Lemon Curd–Filled Ebelskivers

•

Strawberry Shortcake Pancakes

•

Sticky Toffee Ebelskivers

•

Chocolate Truffle Ebelskivers

•

Pumpkin Pie Ebelskivers

•

Ebelskivers, S'mores Style

•

Salted Caramel–Pecan Ebelskivers

•

Molten Chocolate Ebelskivers

# index

# weldon**owen**

415 Jackson Street, Suite 200, San Francisco, CA 94111

Telephone: 415 291 0100 Fax: 415 791 8841

www.wopublishing.com

Weldon Owen is a division of

## BONNIER

### WELDON OWEN INC.

**CEO and President** Terry Newell

**VP, Sales and Marketing** Amy Kaneko

**Director of Finance** Mark Perrigo

**VP and Publisher** Hannah Rahill

**Executive Editor** Jennifer Newens

**Associate Creative Director** Emma Boys

**Art Director** Kara Church

**Senior Designer** Ashley Martinez

**Junior Designer** Anna Grace

**Production Director** Chris Hemesath

**Production Manager** Michelle Duggan

**Color Manager** Teri Bell

### EBELSKIVERS

Conceived and produced by Weldon Owen Inc.

Copyright © 2010 Weldon Owen Inc.

Color separations by Embassy Graphics

Printed and Bound in China by 1010 Printing, Ltd.

First printed in 2010

10 9 8 7 6 5 4 3

Library of Congress Cataloging-in-Publication data is available.

ISBN-13: 978-1-61628-067-3

ISBN-10: 1-61628-067-0

### ACKNOWLEDGMENTS

Weldon Owen wishes to thank the following people for their generous support in producing this book: Charles Ballestamon; Carol Hacker; Julia Humes; Carrie Bradley Neves; Elizabeth Parson; Kate Washington; and Victoria Woolard. Special thanks to the Williams-Sonoma Kitchen for the sticky toffee ebelskiver recipe, which has been adapted for this book.